Christmas Sheet Music

For Piano

Table of Contents

Table of Contents²

1. Angels From The Realms of Glory

James Montgomery

Arrangement & Transcription by Willy Espinoza

Piano

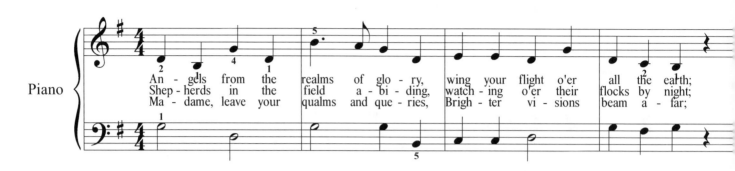

An - gels from the realms of glo - ry, wing your flight o'er all the earth;
Shep - herds in the field a - bi - ding, watch - ing o'er their flocks by night;
Ma - dame, leave your qualms and que - ries, Brigh - ter vi - sions beam a - far;

ye who sang cre - a - tion sto - ry, now pro - claim Mes - si - ah's birth. Go and wor - ship,
God with man is soon re - si - ding; Soon will shine the in - fants Light.
Seek the grat de - sire of na - tions; Ye shall see his __ na - tal star.

Go and wor - ship; wor - ship Christ, the new - born King. Wor - ship Christ the New - born King!

2. Angels We Have Heard On High

Traditional French Song
Arrangement & Transcription by Willy Espinoza

An - gels we have heard on high   Sweet - ly sing - ing o'er the plains   And the moun - tains
Shep - herds, why this ju - bi - lee?   Why your joy - ous strais pro - long?   What the glad - some

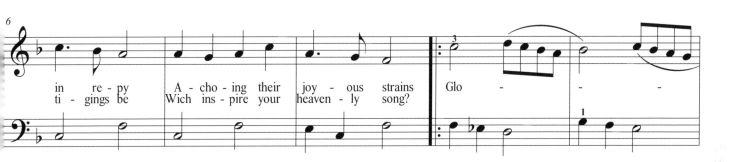

in re - py   A - cho - ing their joy - ous strains   Glo -
ti - gings be   Wich ins - pire your heaven - ly song?

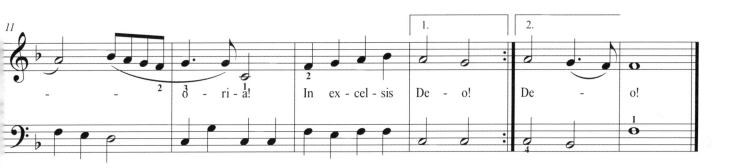

- - ri - a!   In ex - cel - sis De - o!   De - o!

2

3. As with Gladness Men of Old

William Chatterton Dix

Arrangement & Transcription by Willy Espinoza

Piano

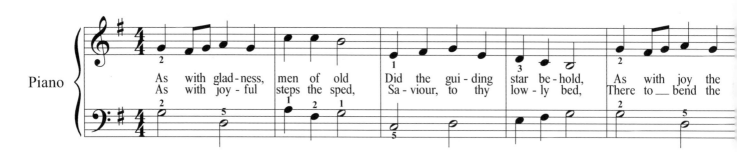

As with glad-ness, men of old
As with joy-ful steps the sped,
Did the gui-ding star be-hold,
Sa-viour, to thy low-ly bed,
As with joy the
There to __ bend the

hailed its light,
knee be-fore
Lead-ing on-ward
The whom hea-ven
beam-ing bright;
and earth adore;
So, most gra-cious
So may we with
Lord, may we
will-ing feet

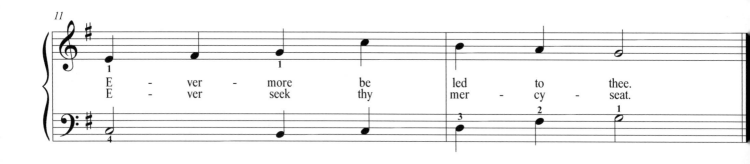

E - ver - more be
E - ver seek thy
led mer - cy - to thee.
seat.

Piano

4. Auld Lang Syne

Doguie McLean

Arrangement & Transcription by Willy Espinoza

Should auld ac-quain-tance be for-got And ne-ver brought to mind? Should

auld ac-quain-tance be for-got And days of auld lang syne? For auld____ lang____

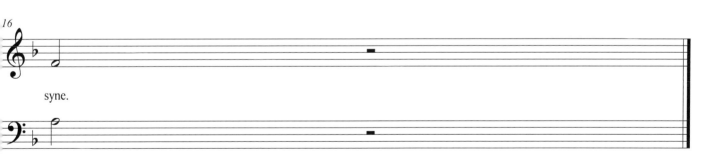

syne, me dear For auld lang syne We'll tak a cup o' kind-ness yet For days of ould lang

syne.

Piano

5. Away in a Manger

Arrangement & Transcription by Willy Espinoza

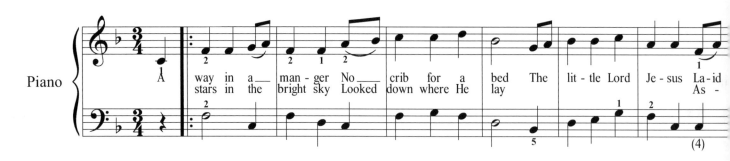

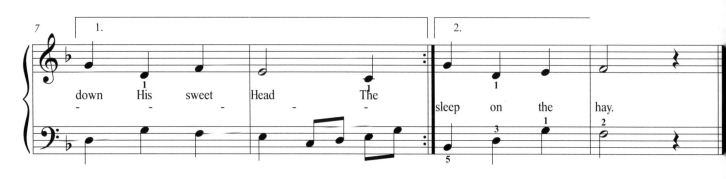

5

6. Bring a Torch, Jeanette Isabella

Loreena McKennitt

Arrangement & Transcription by Willy Espinoza

Bring a torch,___ Jea - nette I - sa - bel - la Bring a torch, to the cra - dle run!
It is wrong when the Child is s - leep - ing It is wrong___ to talk so loud;

It is je - sus, good folk of the vil - lage Christ is born and Ma - ry's cal - ling Ah! ah!
Si - lence, all, as you ga - ther a - round,___ Lest___ your noise should wa - ken Je - sus: Hush! hush!

beau - ti - ful is the mo - ther! Ah! ah! beau - ti - ful is her Son!
see___ how fast He slum - bers: Hush! hush! see___ how fast He sleeps!

7. Christ Was Born On Christmas Day

Arrangement & Transcription by Willy Espinoza

Piano

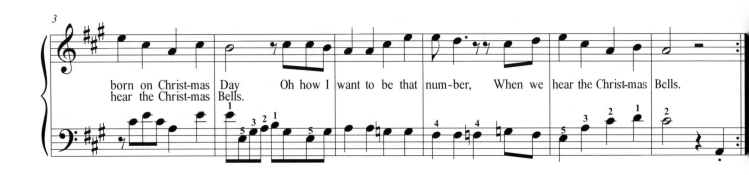

Piano

8. Come, Thou Long-Expected Jesus

Arrangement & Transcription by Willy Espinoza

Piano

Come, Thou long ex - pect - ed Je - sus Born to set Thy peo - ple free; From our fears and

sins re - lease us, Let us find our res in Thee. Is - rael's strength and con - so - la - tion Hope of all __ the

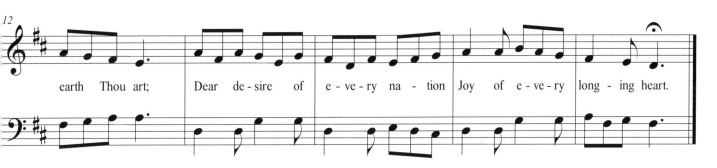

earth Thou art; Dear de - sire of e - ve - ry na - tion Joy of e - ve - ry long - ing heart.

9. The Coventry Carol

Traditional

Arrangement & Transcription by Willy Espinoza

Piano

Lul - ly, lul - la, thou lit - tle ti-ny child, Ba - by, ul - ly lul - lay, thou

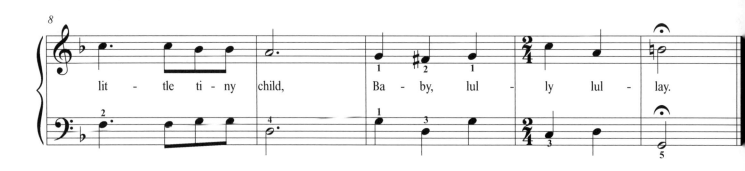

lit - tle ti - ny child, Ba - by, lul - ly lul - lay.

9

10. Deck The Halls

Traditional
Arrangement & Transcription by Willy Espinoza

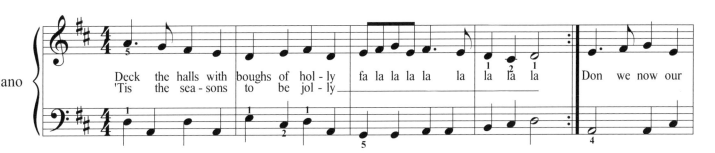

Deck the halls with boughs of hol - ly fa la la la la la la la la Don we now our
'Tis the sea - sons to be jol - ly

gay ap - pa - rel Fa la la la la la la la la Troll the an - cient Yule - tide ca - rol

Fa la la la la la la la la.

11. Ding, Dong Merrily on High

Traditional / Andy Quir

Arrangement & Transcription by Willy Espinoza

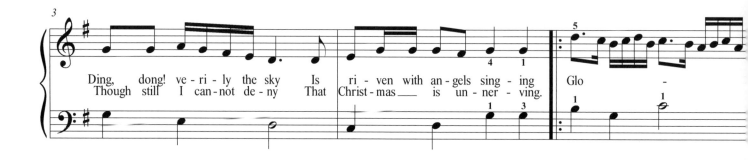

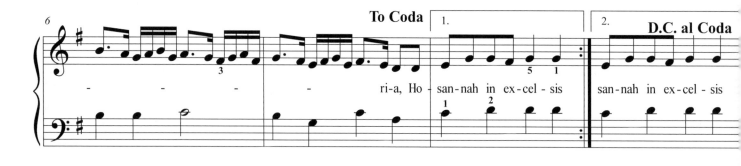

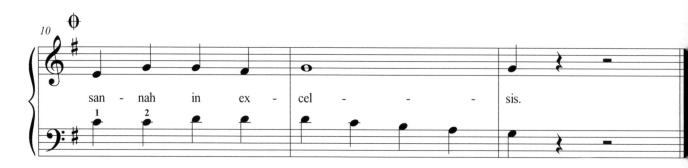

12. Go Tell It On the Mountain

Here We Come A-Caroling

Transcription by Willy Espinoza

13. God Rest Ye Merry, Gentlemen

Traditional

Arrangement & Transcription by Willy Espinoza

Piano

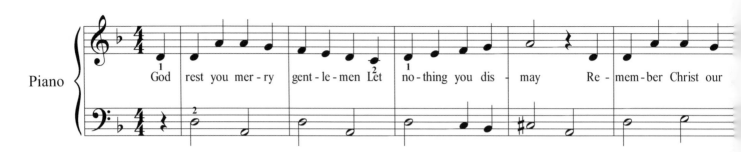

God rest you mer - ry gent - le - men Let no - thing you dis - may Re - mem - ber Christ our

Sa - vior Was born on Christ - mas Day. To save uf all from Sa - tan's pow'r When

we were gone as - tray Oh___ ti - ding of conm - fort and joy Com - fort and joy Oh___

ti - ding of com - fort and joy.

14. Good King Wenceslas

John Mason Neale

Arrangement & Transcription by Willy Espinoza

Piano

Good King Wen - ces - las looked out on the Feast of Ste - phen
Hi - ther, page, and stand by me, if thou knowst it, tel - ling

When the snow lay round a - bout deep and crisp and e - ven Brigh - tly shone the
Yon - der pea - sant who is he?_____ Where and what is dwel - ling? Sire, he lives a

moon that night though the frost was cru - el When a poor man came in sight
good league hence, un - der - neat the moun - tain Right a - gainst the fo - rest fence

gathe - ring win - ter fu - - - el
by Saint Ag - nes foun - - - tain.

15. Hark! The Herald Angel Sings

Music adapted from: "Festgesang" by Felix Mendelssohn,
Arrangement & Transcription by Willy Espinoza

Piano

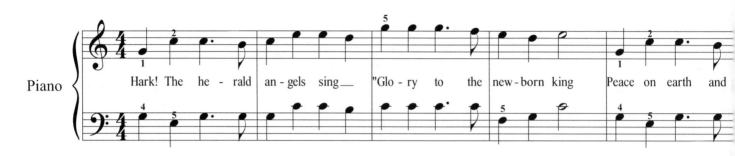

Hark! The he - rald an - gels sing___ "Glo - ry to the new - born king Peace on earth and

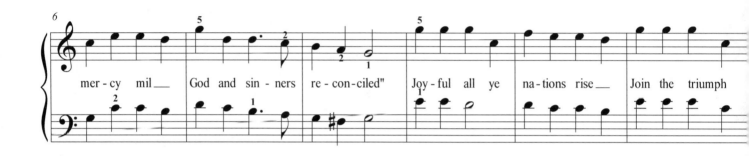

mer - cy mil___ God and sin - ners re - con - ciled" Joy - ful all ye na - tions rise___ Join the triumph

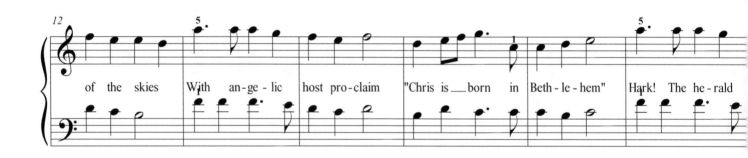

of the skies With an - ge - lic host pro - claim "Chris is___ born in Beth - le - hem" Hark! The he - rald

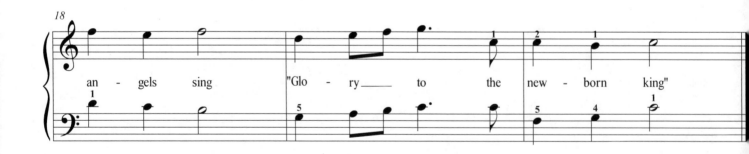

an - gels sing "Glo - ry___ to the new - born king"

15

Piano

16. I Heard the Bells on Christmas Day

Traditional

Arrangement & Transcription by Willy Espinoza

I heard the bells on Christ - mas day Their old fa - mi - liar ca - rols play And

And in des - pair I bowed my head "There is no peace on Earth," I said For

mild and sweet their songs re - peat Of peace on Earth, good will to men.

hate is strong and mocks the song

Piano

17. I Saw Three Ships

The Chieftains
Arrangement & Transcription by Willy Espinoza

Piano

I saw three ships come sail - ing in On Christ - mas day, on Christ - mas day, I
what was in those ships all three, And

saw three ships come sail - ing in On Christ - mas day in the mor - ning? And
what was in those ships all three,

1. mor - ning.
2.

18. In the Bleak Midwinter

Traditional
Arrangement & Transcription by Willy Espinoza

In the bleak mid - win - ter Fros - ty wind made moan Earth stood hard as

i - ron Wa - ter like a stone Snow had fal - len Snow on Snow___ on snow.

In the bleak mid - win - ter Long,___ long a - go.

18

19. It Came Upon the Midnight Clear

Traditional
Arrangement & Transcription by Willy Espinoza

It came u - pon__ a mid - night clear That glo - rious song__ of old. From an - gels bend - ding near the earth to touch their harps of gold. Peace on the earth, good will to men From hea - ven's all gra - cious King The world in so - lemn still - ness lay To hear the an - - - gels sing.

20. Jingle Bells

Traditional
Arrangement & Transcription by Willy Espinoza

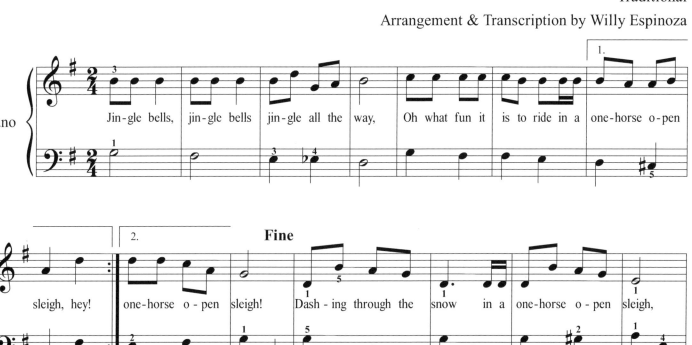

Jin-gle bells, jin-gle bells jin-gle all the way, Oh what fun it is to ride in a one-horse o-pen

sleigh, hey! one-horse o-pen sleigh! Dash-ing through the snow in a one-horse o-pen sleigh,

O'er the fielda we go, laugh-ing all the way Bells on bob-tails ring, Ma-king spi-rits bright. What

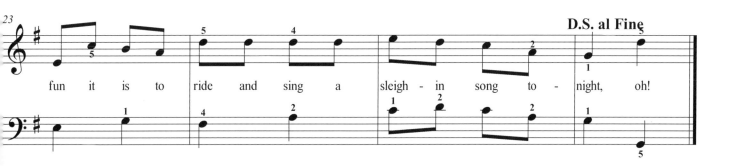

fun it is to ride and sing a sleigh - in song to - night, oh!

Fine

D.S. al Fine

21. Jolly Old St. Nicholas

Traditional

Arrangement & Transcription by Willy Espinoza

Piano

Jol - ly old St. Ni - cho - las
Christ-mas Eve is com - ing soon

Lean your ear this way
Now, you dear old man

Don't you tell a sin - gle soul
Whis - per what you'll bring to me

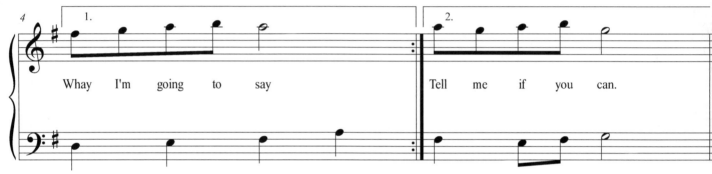

1.
Whay I'm going to say

2.
Tell me if you can.

22. Joy to the World

Isaac Watts

Arrangement & Transcription by Willy Espinoza

Joy to the world, the Lord is come Let Earth re-ceive her King.   Let e - very heart ___ pre-

pare Him room ___ And Hea-ven and na - ture sing   And hea-ven and na - ture sing   And

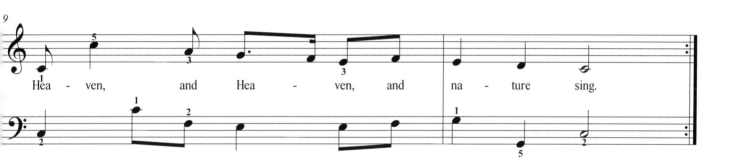

Hea - ven,   and   Hea - ven,   and   na - ture   sing.

23. Il Est Ne

Traditional

Transcription by Willy Espinoza

Piano

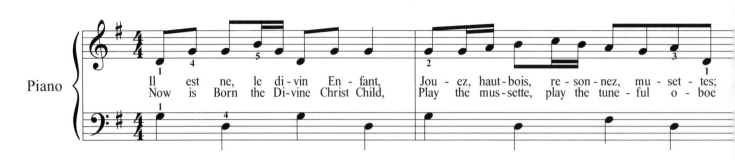

Fine

D.C. al Fine

Piano

24. O Christmas Tree

Arrangement & Transcription by Willy Espinoza

O Christ-mas Tree, O Christ-mas Tree, How faith-ful are thy bran-ches! O Christ-mas Tree, O

Christ-mas Tree, How faith-ful are thy bran-ches! Green nos a-lone in sum-mer-time, But in the win-ter's

frost and rime; O Christ-mas Tree O Christ-mas Tree, How faith-ful are they bran-ches.

24

25. O Come All Ye Faithful

Here We Come A-Caroling

Traditional

Transcription by Willy Espinoza

Piano

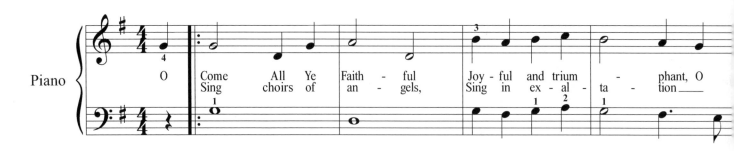

O Come All Ye Faith - ful, Joy - ful and trium - phant, O
Sing choirs of an - gels, Sing in ex - al - ta - tion ___

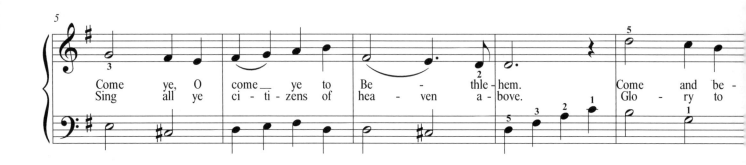

Come ye, O come ye to Be - thle - hem. Come and be
Sing all ye ci - ti - zens of hea - ven a - bove. Glo - ry to

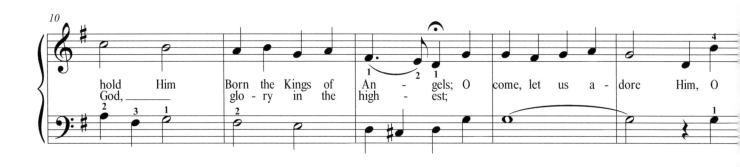

hold Him Born the Kings of An - gels; O come, let us a - dore Him, O
God, ___ glo - ry in the high - est;

come, let us a - dore Him O come, let us a - dore Him, Christ, ___ the Lord.

25

26. O Come, Little Children

Suzuki

Arrangement & Trascription by Willy Espinoza

Piano

27. O Come, O Come, Emmanuel

Arrangement & Transcription by Willy Espinoza

28. O Holy Night

Adolphe Adam

Arrangement & Transcription by Willy Espinoza

29. O Little Town of Bethlehem

Phillips Brooks (1868)

Arrangemen & Transcription by Willy Espinoza

O lit - tle town of Beth - le - hem How still we see thee lie A bove thy deep and

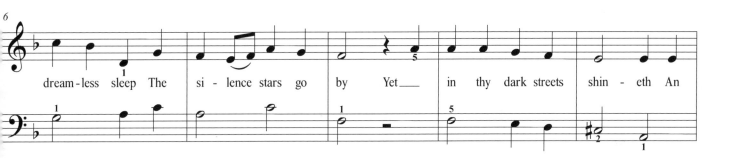

dream - less sleep The si - lence stars go by Yet___ in thy dark streets shin - eth An

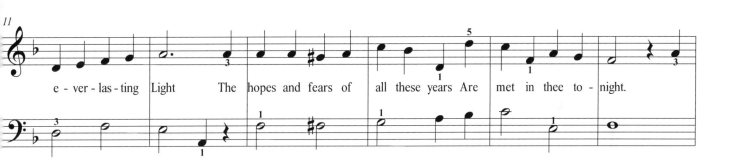

e - ver - las - ting Light The hopes and fears of all these years Are met in thee to - night.

si - len - tly, how si - len - tly The won - drous Goft is given As God im - parts to hu - man hearts The

30. Once in Royal David's City

Arrangament & Transcription by Willy Espinoza

Piano

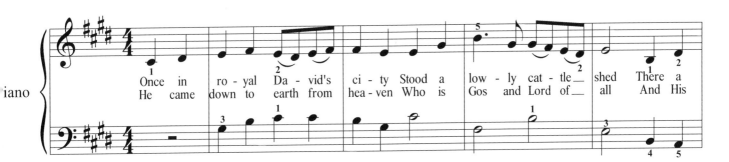

31. Pat-a-Pan

Julie Andrews

Arrangement & Transcription by Willy Espinoza

Piano

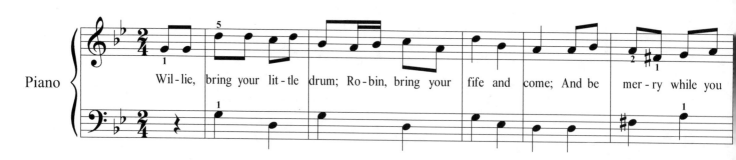

Wil-lie, bring your lit-tle drum; Ro-bin, bring your fife and come; And be mer-ry while you

play tu-re-lu-re - lu pat-a-pan-a- pan, Come be mer-ry while you play, Let us make our Christ-mas day!

32. Silent Night

Franz Xaver Gruber

Arrangement & Transcription by Willy Espinoza

Si – lent night, ho – ly night! All is calm, all is bright!

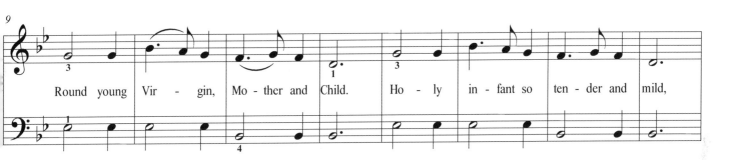

Round young Vir – gin, Mo – ther and Child. Ho – ly in – fant so ten – der and mild,

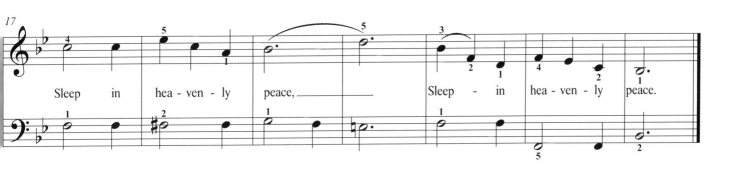

Sleep in hea – ven – ly peace, Sleep – in hea – ven – ly peace.

33. The First Noel

Traditional
Arrangament & Transcription by Willy Espinoza

The | first___ No - el, the | An - gels did say | Was to | cer - tain poor | she - pherds in
fields___ where they | lay | keep - ing their | sheep | On a | coold win - ters' | night___ that

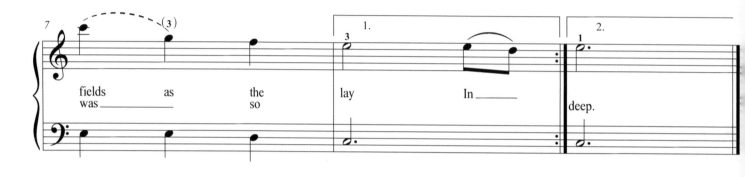

fields as the | lay | In _____
was _____ so | | deep.

34. The Friendly Beasts

Traditional
Arrangement & Transcription by Willy Espinoza

Je - sus   our   bro - ther,   strong   and   good   Was   humb - ly   born ___ in   a   sta - ble   rude   And   the   friend - ly   beasts   a - round   his ___ stood   Je - sus   our   bro - ther,   strong _____ and   good.

35. The Holly and the Ivy

Traditional
Arrangement & Transcription by Willy Espinoza

Piano

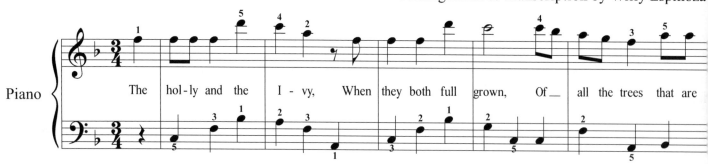

The hol-ly and the I - vy, When they both full grown, Of __ all the trees that are

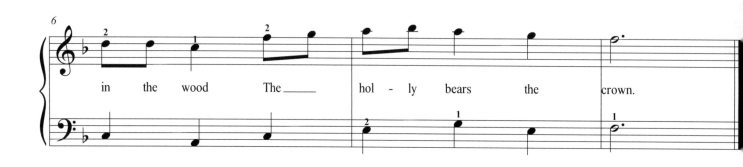

in the wood The ____ hol - ly bears the crown.

36. Up on the Housetop

Benjamin Hanby

Arrangement & Transcription by Willy Espinoza

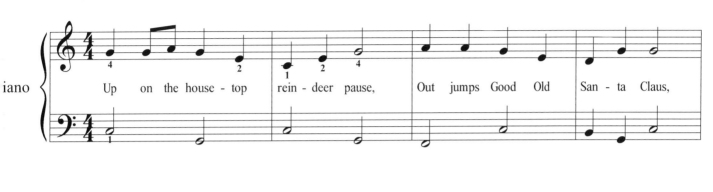

Up on the house-top rein-deer pause, Out jumps Good Old San-ta Claus,

Down through the chim-ney with lots of toys, All for the lit-tle ones Christ-mas joys.

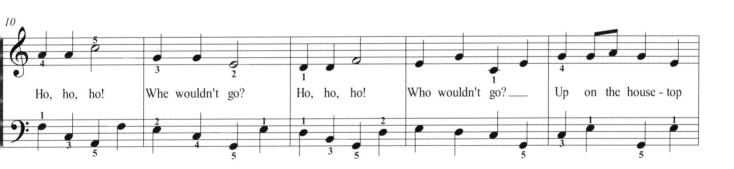

Ho, ho, ho! Whe wouldn't go? Ho, ho, ho! Who wouldn't go? __ Up on the house-top

click, click, click! Down through the chim-ney with good Saint Nick.

Piano

37. We Three Kings Of Orient Are

Traditional

Arrangement & Transcription by Willy Espinoza

Piano

We three kings of o - ri - ent are   Bear - ing gifts we tra - vers a - far   Field and foun - tain

Moor and moun-tain   Fol - lo - wing yon - der star   O____ star of won - der, star of night   Star with ro - yal

beau - ty bright   West - ward lea - ding, still   pro - cee - ding   Guide us to thy   per - fect light.

Piano

38. We Wish You a Merry Christmas

Traditional

Arrangement & Transcription by Willy Espinoza

Piano

We wish you a mer-ry Christ-mas we wish you a mer-ry Christ-mas we wish you a mer-ry

Christ-mas and a hap-py new year Good ti-dings we bring to you and your kin We

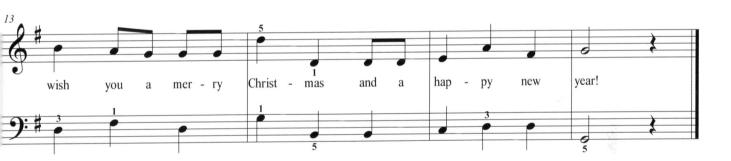

wish you a mer-ry Christ-mas and a hap-py new year!

40

39. What Child Is This?

Traditional
Arrangement & Transcription by Willy Espinoza

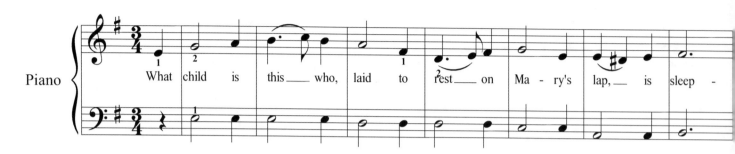

What child is this __ who, laid to rest __ on Ma - ry's lap, __ is sleep -

ing? Whom An - gels greet __ with an - thems sweet __ while shep - herds watch are keep -

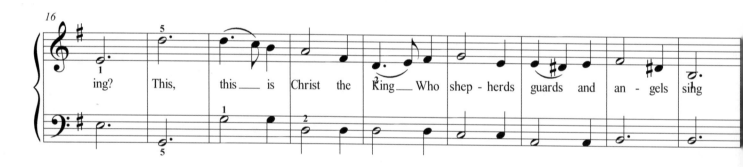

ing? This, this __ is Christ the King __ Who shep - herds guards and an - gels sing

Haste, haste __ to bring him Lord __ The Babe, __ the Son __ of Ma - ry.

40. While Shepherds Watched Their Flocks

Arrangement & Transcription by Willy Espinoza

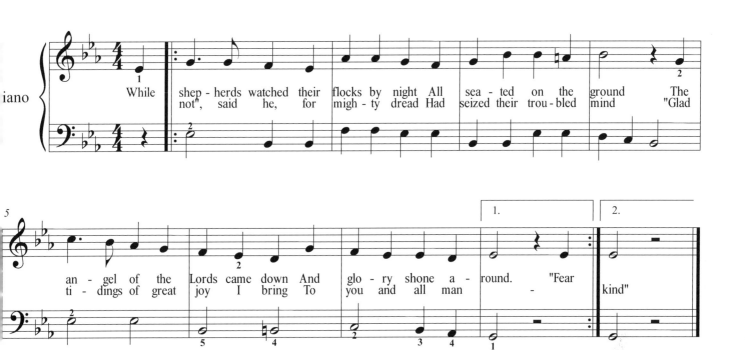

While / not", said he, for

shep-herds watched their flocks by night All seated on the ground The "Glad
mighty dread Had seized their troubled mind

an-gel of the Lords came down And glory shone a-round. "Fear
ti-dings of great joy I bring To you and all man

kind"

41. Rudolph The Red Nosed Reindeer.

Traditional
Arrangement & Transcription by Willy Espinoza

Piano

nose so bright,   Won't you guide my   sleigh to - night?"   The how the rein - deer   loved him.

as they shout-ed out with glee: "Ru-dolph the Red-Nosed Rein-deer,   You'll go down in his-to - ry."

42. Carol of the Bells

Traditional
Arrangement & Transcription by Willy Espinoza

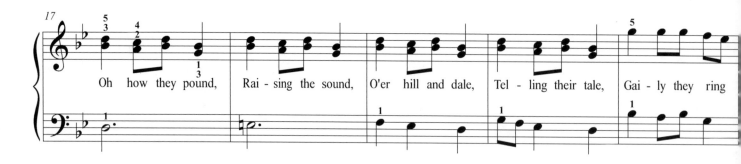

While peo-ple sing   Songs of good   cheer Christ-mas is here   mer - ry,   mer - ry,   mery - ry   mer - ry Christ - mas

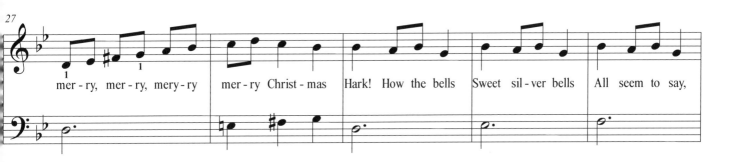

mer - ry,   mer - ry,   mery - ry   mer - ry Christ - mas   Hark! How the bells   Sweet sil - ver bells   All seem to say,

"Throw   care   a - way"

43. Little Drummer Boy

Traditional
Arrangement & Transcription by Willy Espinoza

Piano

Come they told me pa rum pum pum pum. A new born King to

see pa rum pum pum pum. Our fi - nest gifts we bring pa rum pum pum pum.

To set be - fore the King pa rum pum pum pum, rum pum pum pum, rum pum pum

pum pum So to ho - nor Him, pa rum pum pum pum Whenwe come. rum pum pum

pum, rum pum pum pum.

44. Sing We Now of Christmas

Here We Come A-Caroling

Transcription by Willy Espinoza

Sing we now of Christ - mas
An - gels called to shep - herds

No - ël, sing we here!
"Leave your flocks at rest

Hear our grate - ful prai - ses
Jour - ney forth to Bet - hle - hem

To the babe so dear
Find the ba - by blest"

Sing we No - ël, The King is born, No - ël!

Sing we now of Christ - mas, sing we now No - ël!

48

45. The Seven Joys Of Mary

Traditional
Arrangement & Transcription by Willy Espinoza

The first good job that Ma - ry had, it was the joy of one. To see her own son,

Je - sus Christ. when he was first her son. When he was first her son, good man, and bless-ed may he

be _____ Oh_____ Fa - ther, Son and Ho - ly Ghost for all e - ter - ni - ty.

46. Alle Jahre Wieder

Traditional
Arrangement & Transcription by Willy Espinoza

Piano

E - very sin - gle   ye - ar   Ba - by-Christ come a - gain.   Down   to   the

Earth_____   Where   all___   peo - ple   are.

47. Twelve days of Christmas

Arrangement & Transcription by Willy Espinoza

Piano

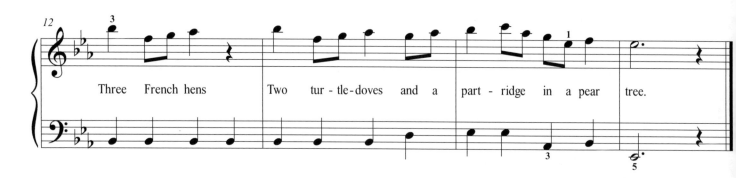

Piano

48. Let it Snow

Frank Sinatraa

Arrangement & Transcription by Willy Espinoza

iano

Oh, the wea-ther out - side is fright - ful but the fire is so de - light - ful. And

since we've no place to go Let it snow, let it snow, let it snow.

49. Ich Steh an Deiner Krippen Hie

ohann Sebastian Bach

Arrangement & Transcription by Willy Espinoza

Piano

I stand be - fore Thy man - ger fair, My Je - sus, Life from Hea - ven I

come, and un - to Thee I bear What Thou to me hast gi - ven. Re - ceive it, for 'tis

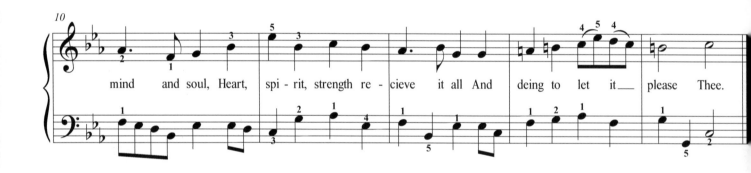

mind and soul, Heart, spi - rit, strength re - cieve it all And deing to let it___ please Thee.

Piano

50. Maria durch ein' Dornwald ging

Traditional

Arrangement & Transcription by Willy Espinoza

Ma - ri - a durch ein Dorn - wald ging Ky - ri-e e-lei - son Ma -

ri - a durch ein Dorn - wald ging Der hat in sie - ben Jahr'n kein Laub ge-tra - gen

Je - sus und Ma - ri - a.

51. I'm a Little Star

Traditional
Arrangement & Transcription by Willy Espinoza

Piano

I'm a lit-tle star,   hang-ing on a tree   See the li-tle chil-dres dance a-round me
I'm a can-dy stick
I'm a pret-ty an - gel

tra - la - la tra - la - la tra - la - la tra - la - la tra - la - la tra - la - la tra - la - la la.

52. In France they have Pere Noel

Arrangement & Transcription by Willy Espinoza

53. Ring Ring Ring The Bells

Traditional
Arrangement & Transcription by Willy Espinoza

Ring, ring, ring the bells, Ring them loud and clear To tell the chil - dren e - very-where That

Christ - mas time is here Ring, ring, ring the bells, Ring them loud and clear To

tell the chil - dren e - very-where That Christ - mas time is here

54. Long Time Ago On Bethlehem

Traditional

Arrangement & Transcription by Willy Espinoza

Long time a-go in Beth - le - hem, so the Ho - ly bi - ble say

Ma - rys boy child Je - sus Christ was born on Christ-mas day.

Hark now hear the

an - gels sing a King was born to - day

And man will live for e - ver more Be -

cause of Christ - mas day!

55. Frosty the Snowman

Traditional
Arrangement & Transcription by Willy Espinoza

Piano

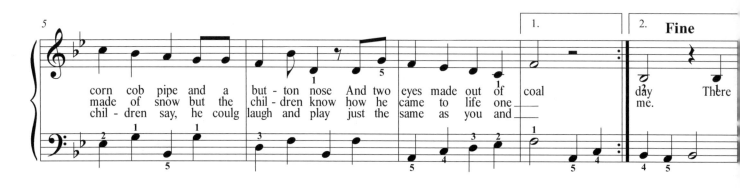

59

56. Christmas in the old man's hat

Traditional

Arrangement & Transcription by Willy Espinoza

57. I Want a Hippopotamus for Christmas

Traditional
Arrangement & Transcription by Willy Espinoza

58. Santa Claus is Coming To Town

Traditional

Arrangement & Transcription by Willy Espinoza

You bet-ter watch out you bet-ter not cry You bet-ter not pout I'm
ma-king a list He's check-ing it twice He's gon-na find out Who's

tel - ling you why San - ta Claus is com-ming' to town. He's
naugh-ty or nice

He sees you when you're sleep-ing He knows when you're a - wake He

know if you've been bad or good So be good for good - ness sakes _____

59. Here Comes Santa Claus

Traditional
Arrangement & Transcription by Willy Espinoza

Piano

60. It's the Most Wonderful Time of the Year

Andy Williams

Arrangement & Transcription by Willy Espinoza

Prestissimo

iano

It's the most won-der-ful time _____ of the year _____ With the
It's the hap - hap-pi-est sea - son of all _____ With those

kids jin - gle bell - ing, and ev - ry' - one tell - ing you, "Be of good cheer." _____
hol - li - day greet - ings, and gay hap - py meet - ings when friends come to call _____

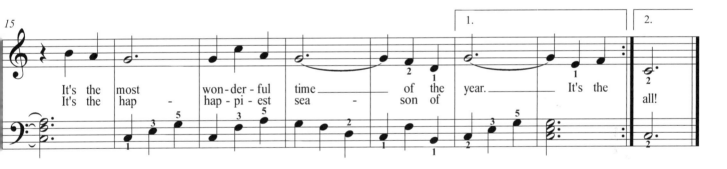

It's the most won-der - ful time _____ of the year. _____ It's the
It's the hap - hap - pi - est sea - son of

1.

It's the

2.

all!

64

Made in the USA
Monee, IL
19 November 2024

70533880R30037